The Advanced
Iron Palm
By Master Brian Gray

The Advanced
Iron Palm

UNIQUE PUBLICATIONS

DISCLAIMER

Although both Unique Publications and the author(s) of this martial arts book have taken great care to ensure the authenticity of the information and techniques contained herein, we are not responsible, in whole or in part, for any injury which may occur to the reader or readers by reading and/or following the instructions in this publication. We also do not guarantee that the techniques and illustrations described in this book will be safe and effective in a self-defense or training situation. It is understood that there exist a potential for injury when using or demonstrating the techniques herein described. It is essential that before following any of the activities, physical or otherwise, herein described, the reader or readers first should consult his or her physician for advice on whether practicing or using the techniques described in this publication could cause injury, physical or otherwise. Since the physical activities described herein could be too sophisticated in nature for the reader or readers, it is essential a physician be consulted. Also, federal, state or local laws may prohibit the use or possession of weapons described herein. A thorough examination must be made of the federal, state and local laws before the reader or readers attempts to use these weapons in a self-defense situation or otherwise. Neither Unique Publications nor the author(s) of this martial arts book guarantees the legality or the appropriateness of the techniques or weapons herein contained.

Copyright © 1995 by Unique Publications
All rights reserved.
Printed in the United States of America

ISBN: 0-86568-159-7
Library of Congress Catalog No.: 94-061145

4201 Vanowen Place
Burbank, California 91505

Contents

Foreword   9

Chapter One
How to Make Dit Da Jow   11

Chapter Two
Disturbances to the Spine   44

Chapter Three
Translation of the Famous Woodcuts from the Hsi Yuan Chi Lu   49

Chapter Four
Meditation – The Secrets of the Sacred   90

Foreword

I have divided my iron palm material into two books. The first installment was The Complete Iron Palm, while the second is Advanced Iron Palm. The reason was simple: I wanted a manual for the iron palm student which would deal with getting the hands ready, a task which should take a minimum of three years. And I wanted that book to solely concentrate on that aspect.

The second book will take the student into actual methods of application and higher-level techniques.

This book contains recipes for making dit da jow, techniques on how to increase your power, anatomical descriptions of the do ming dien mo or fatal striking, and several self-defense applications involving the palm.

After reading both books, you should be armed to fight the vast array of frauds out there who are ready to take your money and give you nothing in return.

Remember to train diligently, avoid violence, and always stand out for justice. Avoiding violence does not mean never using your power, but, as I often tell my students, "A man's kung-fu prowess is like his underwear; both should be displayed with equal discretion."

When you have completed the training these books describe, your hands will be deadlier than ever before. With that knowledge comes a great responsibility. However, I am confident anyone willing to spend three years preparing the hand has the necessary discipline to know when and when not to use it.

Chapter One
How to Make Dit Da Jow

There are coutntless recipes for dit da jow, which often surprises many beginners. The key is to understand that dit da jow is merely an adjective and not a product name, much like the word "toothpaste". When you think of toothpaste, you may think of a specific brand, and while one may have more abrasives for cleaning, and another may have more breath freshners, in the end they are still called "toothpaste". So it is with dit da jow. The brands available range in both strength and color; some so weak the affects are negligible to some so potent that you can watch a bruise literally disappear on contact.

Dit da jow is a collection of herbs specially prepared in a base of wine. In this liquid, you could put anywhere from three or four, to a hundred different herbs, and it would still be dit da jow as long as the ingredients prevented blood stagnation, promoted blood circulation, tonified the blood, and reduced pain and swelling induced by trauma. There are a large number of these herbs, so, for practical purposes, only a few are used in any given recipe.

People who claim their recipe is the best because they have more herbs are being foolish. It is not the number of herbs, but the specific combination of certain herbs that makes a superior liniment. When someone maintains his recipe is better, he should be willing to supply scientific evidence backing up his claim. Simply quoting numbers, such as 20 versus 10, is as foolish as saying bread made with more ingredients automatically makes it better or more wholesome. We all know this is not necessarily so.

Tonal Level Chart

Voice Line — Tonal Level One—Voice stays the same

Tonal Level Two—Voice goes up two steps

Tonal Level Three—Voice drops, then rises two steps

Tonal Level Four—Voice drops two steps

To better understand dit da jow, first, let's do some translating. The two most popular dialects of Chinese used in the United States are Cantonese and Mandarin. The words "dit da jow", are Cantonese; for Mandarin one says, "Tieh Da Jiu". Tone levels are important in Chinese, since a given word may be pronounced the same as several other words, but the tonal level will change its meaning; thus, the wrong tonal level will change a speaker's meaning.

For example, , the word "yee" can mean the number "one", or it can mean "mind", simply depending on which of four tonal levels one uses. So, if you want to buy dit da jow at a Chinese herb shop, knowing how to pronounce it will get you off to a good start. Tonal levels are similar in sound to what we call inflection, that is, the way we raise or lower the emphasis on certain parts of a word, or sentence, to change the meaning.

An example is the word, "Yeah". Yeah? is spoken differently from Yeah! In the first one, Yeah?, we raise the voice two steps. In the second, we lower the voice two steps, Yeah! Consider the accompanying level chart and final tonal level three. That is the tonal level for each of the three words comprising dit da jow. Since you would sound funny saying three third tonal levels in a row, on the words "dit da" you make the two words receive only one tonal level, and the word "jow" receives an individual tonal level. Thus, you pronounce the words this way:

DIT   DA   JOW   TIEH   DA   JIU

I have written these words in character form so you may learn to write them. Dit, or tieh, means "iron." Da, means "hit", and jow, or jiu, means "wine". Thus, dit da jow means "iron hit wine", a liniment based in wine that is used in the striking practice of the iron palm and other iron incorporating practices. While it is easier to buy already-packaged dit da jow, some people prefer—even enjoy—making their own, so let's see what's in store for those who want to put their personal stamp on dit da jow.

Once you have selected the herbs—we will discuss which herbs to use later—crush them into a coarse powder. Place one ounce of each herb into a large, non-metallic cooking pot, and add one quart of vodka. Simmer slowly over a low fire for three and a half hours. Remove from heat and pour the contents into a two-gallon jar along with six quarts of vodka. Seal the mixture in an air-tight jar. Store this mixture in a cool, dark area (basements are perfect) for at least two months and preferably one year; the longer it ages, the more potent it becomes.

	Mandarin	Cantonese
鐵	T'ieh*	Dit

*(Tieh is also written this way)

	Mandarin	Cantonese
掌	Da	Da
	Jiu	Jow

Some people vary the ounces of herb they use per gallon of dit da jow. Most recipes call for between three-fifths of an ounce to two ounces per gallon. Also, some recipes will vary the ounces from herb to herb. One may call for one ounce of Tien Ch'i yet two ounces of Ru Hsiang, or vice versa. You are free to experiment, but remember, there are basically three types of herbal properties that must be balanced in your recipe. Be careful of having too many of one type. The three types are: those which reduce pain so you can withstand stronger striking practice; those which stimulate blood circulation to help chi flow; and those which break up blood clots that arise from bruising.

Now for the ingredients:

Red Peony Root

Radix Paeonia Rubra —Latin
Ch'ih Shou—Chinese

It is used to remove stagnated blood and eliminate evil heat from blood, for the treatment of pains due to blood stasis, and acute inflammation.

Dragon's Blood

Sanguis Draconis—Latin
Shweh Jin, or Shweh Jie—Chinese

It is used to remove blood stasis, to relieve pains, and to promote the healing of traumatic wounds and bleedings. The drug consists of a red resin secreted from the fruit of Daemonorops draco Blume.

Cat-Tail Pollen

Pollen Typhae—Latin
Pu Huang—Chinese

It is used to promote the circulation of blood and relieve pain by eliminating blood stasis. The carbonized drug is used as hemostatic for various types of bleeding.

Myrrh

Myrrha, Resina Myrrhae—Latin
Mei Yao, or Mo Yao—Chinese

It is used to relieve pain and swelling due to blood stasis or trauma.

Root of Pseudoginseng

Gynura Pinatifida
Radix Pseudoginseng—Latin
T'ien Ch'i—Chinese

It prevents blood stasis by breaking up blood clots and stopping internal bleeding.

Safflower

Flos Carthami—Latin
Hung Hua—Chinese

It is used to stimulate blood flow and relieve pain by removing stagnated blood. It also removes the pain of traumatic wounds, and is used for treatment of painful swellings due to blood stasis.

Frankincense

Mastix, Olibanum,
Resina Olibani,
Boswellia Glabra—Latin
Ru Hsiang—Chinese

It is used to relive pain and swelling by invigorating blood circulation, for the treatment of pains due to blood stasis, and traumatic pains.

Chinese Angelica Root

Radix Angelicae Sinensis—Latin
Dang Gwei—Chinese

It is used to nourish the blood and to invigorate the blood circulation.

Aucklandia Root

Radix Saussurae lappae Clarke
Radix Aucklandiae
Aucklandia lappa Decne.—Latin

It is used as a pain reliever and an antispasmodic.

The nine herbs listed above can be used to make a very potent dit da jow. Moreover, they are non-poisonous, so no harm will come if they are ingested. But the following herbs, when added to the previous nine, are poisonous and will produce an even more potent formula. Therefore, when making your dit da jow, you must decide on a non-poisonous or poisonous formula. If you choose the poisonous route, be sure to keep the lotion out of cuts and away from your mouth.

Peach Kernel

Prunus Persica—Latin
Tao Ren—Chinese

Promotes circulation and dissolves clots.

Clove Tree

Syzygium Aromaticum
Flos Caryophylli
Eugenia Caryophyllata—Latin
Ding Xiang—Chinese

The oil of the cloves is an excellent local anesthetic; the drug promotes circulation.

Rhubarb

Rheum Officinale
Radix et Rhizoma Rhei—Latin
Da Huang—Chinese

Removes blood stagnation caused by traumatic injury. Applied to burns, the powdered herb relieves pain and swelling.

Borneo Camphor Tree

Dryobalanops Aromatica
Dryobalanops Camphora
Borneolum—Latin

Lung Nao Xiang
Bing Pian—Chinese

It is used as an aromatic for the treatment of loss of consciousness. Reduces edema and alleviates pain.

Horse Coin or Horse Money

Ma Ch'ien—Chinese

This herb remains somewhat of a mystery since I can't find a Latin definition. It is the most poisonous herb I've listed, and I was taught that it makes the dit da jow much more potent by its presence. I was told by one Oriental friend that if you want to gain true strength, you take this herb internally, after you have prayed to the gods, and if you do not die, then you will be very strong; also impotent. Thanks, but I will stick to using it externally.

   Note: According to a kind gentleman by the name of Stuart Mauro, O.M.D., who wrote me, the Latin name for this herb is Semen Strychnos Nux Vomica. It arouses spirit, eliminates accumulated swellings, and controls pain.

Glossary of Terms

Abdominal distention—A condition in which the abdomen is blown out or enlarged.

Amenorrhea—The absence of menstrual periods.

Angina pectoris—Pain in the chest coming on after mild or severe exercise or excitement. It is due to local mechanical obstruction of the arteries that supply the heart with blood. The result of this poor blood supply is that the heart muscle cramps, which causes the pain.

Anodyne—A pain-relieving drug.

Antispasmodic—Something which relieves muscular spasm.

Blood Stasis—Cessation of the flow of blood.

Carminative—A drug employed to have a soothing effect on the stomach.

Cholecystalgia—Biliary colic. Biliary colic is severe paroxysmal pain due to the passage of a gallstone through the cystic and common bile ducts of the gall bladder. (Paroxysm—A sudden onset of a disease or of any symptoms, especially if they are recurrent, as in malaria. A spasm, convulsion.)

Dysmenorrhea—Excessively painful menstruation.

Emollient—A soothing or a softening preparation.

Epistaxis—Nose bleeding, nasal hemorrhage.

Gastralgia—Pain in the stomach.

Hematemesis—The vomiting of blood.

Hematuria—The presence of blood in the urine.

Hemoptysis—Spitting up of blood. This may occur in conditions such as bronchitis or a catarrhal cold, or it may be the first sign of a growth in the lung or of active tuberculosis. Sometimes, however, the blood does not come from the lungs but from the back of the throat.

Hemostatic—Arresting bleeding.

Hepatomegaly—Enlargement of the liver.

Menorrhagia—Excessively profuse menstruation.

Splenomegaly—Enlargement of the spleen.

Tenesmus—A painful straining, particularly a painful straining effort to empty the bladder, or bowel, usually without success.

Dit da jow is not used solely for iron palm practice. It is a medication with numerous uses, all relating to the blood. Next to each herb I have given the function of each ingredient in the recipe. These various functions are what can be obtained from using this dit da jow formula when applied to affected areas. Consider a personal incident.

A scratch I received while playing with one of my dogs became infected. Although I cleansed the scratch, I should have disinfected it. However, it was small and no problem. When a boil erupted, I finally took notice and lanced it, removing the pus and cleaning the wound. A few days later, the wound was still infected, and the boil was again growing. I lanced the boil again, removed the pus, cleansed the wound, and waited for it to heal. The next day, the skin around the boil was bruised in a circle about four inches wide. I was bothered by this latest development, so I decided to help get the blood circulating and rejuvenating around the wounded area by applying dit da jow.

The next day, the bruising was gone and the boil was much smaller. Several days later there was no trace of a problem. I know the herbs in this recipe promoted a break-up of the blood that was stagnating in the boil by increasing the circulation in the immediate area. As you can see, by studying the functions of the various herbs, you will find more uses for your dit da jow.

Generating the Wave

Side View *Front View*

In this series of photos, Richard Smalley, a student of Master Gray's, demonstrates the motions inherent in the practice of "Generating the Wave".

Begin in a forward bow and arrow stance with the hands in the position of forward pushing palms.

Side View *Front View*

Rock back into a reverse bow and arrow stance while pulling down and back on the wrists. The wrists lead, the fingers follow. Imagine a wave of force now originating at the toes and beginning to follow a path up the leg.

Side View *Front View*

Notice the stance is rising on the back leg, going from a low to high stance, thus drawing a circle with the movement. When you go from the first to last move, you will have drawn back, down, up, forward, and down, completing this circle. Imagine the force coming up through the torso as the hands, pulling at the wrists, rise to shoulder height.

Side View *Front View*

You now are riding the wave forward. As the wrists reach shoulder height, push forward on the wrists and imagine the force coming up the back, over the shoulders and down through the arms. Complete the stance by riding forward higher than you will be for your ending stance.

Side View *Front View*

In this final photo, the force of the wave has reached the palms, and you are in a forward bow and arrow stance. Imagine the force reaching the palms just as you reach your ending position.

Single Palm

Photo 1

Photo 2

In striking with the single palm, the method of "Generating the Wave for the Single Palm" is shown in this series of photos. Always keep in mind that as you advance in your training, the size of the circle should decrease in size, yet still contain the power of the larger circle used by the beginner. Photo 1 shows the beginning posture. Photo 2 shows dropping to a back stance and imagining the force coming up the legs to the hips.

Photo 3 *Photo 4*

Photo 3 shows the force reaching the hips, at which point you amplify the force by twisting the hips forward, sending the force up the side of the torso and into the shoulders. Photo 4 shows the force now being sent into the arm.

Photo 5   *Photo 6*

In photo 5, imagine the force is traveling down the arm to the palm literally in a wave action. In photo 6, the impacting moment.

Self-Defense Applications (1)

Photo 1 *Photo 2*

In photo 1, I block the incoming fist with my left hand and immediately change the block into a grasp. In photo 2, while steering the fist in the direction it was going, I step slightly into my opponent while continuing to pull him past me.

Photo 3 *Photo 4*

In photo 3, I absorb the opponent's fist force and redirect it as if I were doing the exercise of "Generating the Wave of the Single Palm". I prepare to strike. In photo 4, I strike a point directly on top of the head called Bai Hwei, the One Hundred Meeting Point. Striking this point with the iron palm can be fatal.

Self-Defense Applications (2)

Photo 1 *Photo 2*

In photo 1, I parry with my right hand as I begin to step into my strike. In photo 2, the circle begun with the block is finished with the strike.

Self-Defense Applications (3)

Photo 1 *Photo 2*

In photo 1, I hook block the incoming kick with my left hand. In photo 2, I strike to one of the two points on the inside of the thigh which will temporarily paralyze the leg from the waist down.

Self-Defense Applications (4)

Photo 1   *Photo 2*

In photo 1, I palm block with my right hand. In photo 2, I bring my left hand up and over and trap my opponent's fist with my left, freeing my right palm to continue forward into a strike.

Photo 3 *Photo 4*

In photo 3, my opponent throws another fist which is blocked by the freed hand on the way into its strike. In photo 4, after executing the block, the palm continues into the strike.

Self-Defense Applications (5)

Photo 1

Photo 2

In photo 1, I block the incoming fist with my left hand. In Photo 2, I turn the block into a tight grasp.

Photo 3

Photo 4

In photo 3, by twisting the opponent's wrist in a counterclockwise turn, I force him over and expose his chest. In photo 4, I deliver the iron palm directly over the heart.

Self-Defense Applications (6)

Photo 1   *Photo 2*

In photo 1, the blocking action is performed by the left hand, while an iron palm strike is applied to my opponent's incoming fist. There are some who are quite capable of shattering an opponent's bones the length of the arm with this strike. In photo 2, this gripping action can be used two ways. One is simply to exert control for redirecting your opponent. The other is to crush the bones in the opponent's fist, a skill only attainable with tremendous training.

Self-Defense Applications (7)

Photo 1

Photo 2

In photo 1, parry the incoming fist with the left palm. In photo 2, while guiding the opponent's fist away from me, I strike to the midsection as I step in.

Self-Defense Applications (8)

Photo 1

Photo 2

In photo 1, I parry the incoming fist with my left hand. In photo 2, turning the block into a grasp, I twist my opponent's wrist in a counterclockwise direction, exposing his back.

Photo 3

The finishing position for the strike to the back.

Self-Defense Applications (9)

Photo 1   *Photo 2*

In photo 1, I block downward against my opponent's incoming fist. In photo 2, stepping forward, I spiral clockwise with my whole arm into my opponent's armpit.

Photo 3 *Photo 4*

In photo 3, by wedging my opponent's arm in the crotch of my elbow, I now have a lever to force him forward and down, exposing the back. In photo 4, the position for the strike to the back.

Chapter Two
Disturbances to the Spine

In discussing the spine, it must be noted that striking the spine can produce wide-ranging effects. These effects range from paralysis to death, from instant to delayed results, and from minor to major pain and discomfort. It is not the spinal bone itself that causes problems, but rather the nerves that are damaged from a well-placed blow. Whether a nerve is severed, or left intact; whether it is hit hard, or light; whether the outer protective sheath is ruptured, or left healthy; all these factors determine the outcome. Some strikes, therefore, will have a degenerative, or "delayed," effect. The spine may be struck now, but the resultant injury might not occur for days. Since a further discussion would only serve to complicate the material I offer here, I am only going to discuss target areas that produce immediate results.

At the top of the spine is the cervical vertebra. There are eight pairs of cervical nerves derived from cord segments located between the level of the foramen magnum and the middle of the seventh cervical vertebra. The first four vertebra form an interjoining of nerves called the cervical plexus. The last four, together with the first thoracic, form the brachial plexus. Located between the cervical and brachial plexus, cervical vertebrae 3, 4, and 5, is the phrenic nerve. Phrenic injury is the most important of all the cervical traumas. The phrenic nerve passes obliquely over the scalenus anterior muscle and between the subclavian artery and vein to enter the thorax behind the sternoclavicular joint where it descends vertically through the superior and middle mediastinum to the diaphragm. If the trauma to this nerve is of sufficient intensity, death will result from respiratory failure.

Moving down the spine to the brachial plexus, cervical 6, 7, 8 and thoracic 1 form the radial, or musculospiral, nerve. The largest branch of the brachial plexus, the radial nerve begins at the lower border of the pectoralis minor as the direct continuation of the posterior cord. During its descent in the arm, it accompanies the profunda artery behind and around the humerus, and in the musculospiral groove. Piercing the lateral intermuscular septum, it reaches the lower anterior side of the forearm where its terminal branches arise. The separating distance between the cervical plexus and the brachial plexus is only fractions of an inch, yet, when we speak of applying the iron palm in an intense strike to the phrenic nerve—causing death—shifting downward to the radial nerve elicits a totally different response: paralysis of the arms. If the intent of the strike is not to kill, then great care must be taken to avoid the area affecting the phrenic nerve.

Striking the radial nerve results in various types of paralysis in the arms, depending on the area of the nerve path struck and the intensity of the trauma. An iron palm strike to the back of the neck could cover the area of the juncture of the cervical and brachial plexuses, causing simultaneous arm paralysis and respiratory failure. To avoid the chance of fatality—if this is not the desired result—it would be easier to interrupt the radial nerve at the axilla (armpit), or at any point along its journey down the arm. For accurate striking, such as knuckle strikes, the sixth cervical segment paralyzes the adductors of the arm and extensors of the forearm. The seventh cervical causes adduction of the arms and flexion of the forearms, due to paralysis of the deltoid and triceps muscles.

There are several more nerves connected to the brachial plexus. They are the long thoracic, suprascapular, dorsal scapular, thoracodorsal, anterior thoracic, medial brachial, antibrachial cutaneous, musculocutaneous, axillary, median, and ulnar. If one wishes to trace the paths of these nerves, a good anatomy book, such as Gray's Anatomy (no relation), will show them well. They all relate, however, to muscles affecting paralysis of the arms.

Moving further down the spine, we come to the thoracic, which is composed of 12 bones. It is only necessary here to deal with the first five vertebrae of the thoracic, since these have a relative influence to the cardiac plexus. Because of its proximity to the medulla, a strike of sufficient force will produce nerve shock and unconsciousness. A strike with a powerful, deep-penetrating force will bring on enough nervous relay to the cardiac plexus to cause cardiac arrest and death. It should be noted here that the cardiac plexus does not originate at the thoracic, but is a branch of the vagus nerve; however, the cardiac plexus is situated in line with these first five thoracic vertebrae.

Next, we come to the lumbar, which is composed of five bones. One of the most important nerves is the femoral, the largest branch of the lumbar plexus. It arises from the three posterior divisions of the plexus, derived from the 2nd, 3rd and 4th lumbar nerves. Emerging from the lateral border of the psoas just above Poupart's ligament, it descends beneath this ligament to enter the femoral trigone on the lateral side of the femoral artery where it divides into terminal branches.

The second most important nerve after the femoral is the obturator, arising from the lumbar plexus by a fusion of the three anterior divisions of the plexus which are derived from the 2nd, 3rd, and 4th lumbar nerves. Emerging from the medial border of the psoas near the brim of the pelvis, it passes on the lateral side of the hypogastric vessels and ureter and descends through the obturator canal in the upper part of the obturator foramen to the medial side of the thigh. In the canal it splits into anterior and posterior branches. A palm strike to the lumbar vertebrae will produce temporary paralysis from the thigh downward and will involve any, if not all, areas relative to the path of these two nerves.

Since the coccyx is relatively unimportant, the terminating point for our discussion of spinal attacks is the sacrum. Here the sciatic nerve, the largest in the body, is formed. It consists of two separate nerves in one sheath; common peroneal, formed by the upper four posterior divisions of the sacral plexus, and the tibial, formed from all five anterior divisions. Leaving the pelvis through the greater sciatic foramen, usually below the piriformis muscle, it descends between the greater trochanter of the femur and the ischial tuberosity along the posterior surface of the thigh to the popliteal space where it terminates by dividing into the tibial and common peroneal nerves. Trauma to the sciatic will cause paralysis of the hamstring, or paralysis of all leg and foot muscles.

Because of the complexity of trying to oversimplify this chapter, I have opted, instead, to keep this chapter medically sound and provide the reader with a list of definitions to those words which may need a more thorough explanation.

Adduction—Movement of a part of the body, usually an arm or a leg, toward the midline.

Adductors—Muscles involved in movement toward the midline.

Anterior—Located in the front.

Deltoid—The broad, flat muscle covering the shoulder. It helps to lift the arm away from the side of the body.

Diaphragm—The muscular partition located between the chest cavity and the abdominal cavity.

Extensors—Muscles which straighten a limb or part.

Femoral trigone—The triangular shaped portion of the femur.

Foramen—An opening in the bones which permits nerves or blood vessels to exit.

Foramen magnum—A great opening in the occipital bone through which the brain and spinal cord are connected.

Flexion—The act of bending or the condition of being bent.

Greater trochanter of the femur—Of the two processes below the neck of the femur, the greater trochanter is located at the outer side.

Hypogastric vessels—Vessels that pertain to the hypogastrium, which is the lower median anterior region of the abdomen.

Ischial tuberosity—At the bottom of the pelvic bone is a part of the bone called the os innominatum. The large, rough emminence on which the trunk rests when sitting is called the ischial tuberosity and is located on the os innominatum.

Lateral intermuscular septum—Lateral means side; intermuscular means between muscles; septum means a dividing wall.

Medial border—Middle border

Medulla—Medulla oblongata; the lowermost portion of the brain just above the beginning of the spinal cord.

Musculospiral groove—Pertaining to muscles and having a spiral direction.

Pectoralis minor—A chest muscle.

Phrenic nerve—The nerve supplying the diaphragm.

Piriformis muscle—A muscle of the thigh.

Plexus—A network of nerves or blood vessels.

Popliteal space—The space behind the knee.

Posterior—Located in the back or rear.

Poupart's ligament—The ligament in the groin extending from the pubic bone to the crest of the hip bone. It marks the division between abdomen and thigh.

Profunda artery—The artery of the upper arm.

Psoas—Muscles of the thigh which flex and rotate the thigh outward.

Scalenus anterior muscle—A muscle which flexes the neck sideways and supports the head.

Sternoclavicular joint—The point where the sternum and clavicle join.

Subclavian artery and vein—Artery and vein situated under the clavicle.

Superior and middle mediastinum—The mediastinum is the space beneath the breastbone containing the heart, aorta, vena cava, trachea, and other vessels and nerves, and superior and middle are regions of the mediastinum.

Thorax—The chest.

Trauma—Injury.

Triceps—The muscle of the upper arm which straightens the elbow.

Ureter—The tube leading from the kidney to the bladder.

Vagus nerve—The tenth cranial nerve. The largest nerve in the body, supplying the heart, lungs and the abdominal organs.

CHAPTER THREE
Translation of the Famous Woodcuts

A translation of the famous woodcuts from the Hsi Yuan Chi Lu, or the collected writings on the Washing Away of Wrongs

Quite often, the charts which follow in this chapter are used by those who attach great mystery to them in the martial arts. Many have wondered what the points mean, and I have seen no translations of these two famous woodcuts anywhere. I, therefore, decided to translate them for this book so those who read this may learn the truth of what is contained on those two pages. This posed no simple task. Many of the words on the charts are severely smudged and broken up.

Also, many of the words are written in a manner no longer used, making it necessary to compare ancient meanings with new ones, old ways of writing with modern modes. In short, it was a very tedious project. I have also tried to print Chinese characters as simply as possible so that those wishing to write them, or learn to write them, would have an easier time than if I had used a more flowing script. However, my printing leaves a lot to be desired, so I apologize to those better than myself, and especially to the Chinese. Their language is too beautiful for me to be wrecking it like this, but if they will forgive me this time, the next time I promise to use my mao bi.

The woodcuts in question come from an ancient book in China, which was used by forensic pathologists around the time it was written in A.D. 1247. In China, homicides were prosecuted as far back as the Ch'in dynasty (221-207 B.C.), and thus deaths were investigated by state order. This collection of writings was called the Hsi Yuan Chi Lu, or The Washing Away of Wrongs, and was designed to help officials who were assigned to investigate suspicious deaths. In the Hsi Yuan Chi Lu, one may find information about vital spots or danger points by noting that those spots marked with a hollow dot are non-fatal, while those marked with a solid dot are fatal. These spots are considered to be of special sensitivity and danger in case of violent assault, where trauma, contusion or shock could lead to internal injury, or death, sometimes with no external sign of wounding.

For example, trauma at the base of the skull can lead to fracture of the odontoid process of the second cervical vertebra, or the transverse process of the first cervical vertebra, accompanied by injury to the vertebral artery and, thus, severe subarachnoid hemorrhages. This would be one of those times when no external signs of damage would be visible after death. By studying this book, one can soon see that it was an invaluable tool to those ancient forensic officials.

I have been very careful in the writing of this book, in that I do not want to simply draw a bunch of charts for readers, mark the exact locations, and give the results of the strikes.

Never.

The difference between a common street hoodlum and a martial artist is that the hoodlum is no scholar. In this chapter, I will be so bold as to diagram and explain a few strikes. The genuine martial artist, however, will merely need to study and do his homework. It is all here.

Pronunciation Key

I use several variations on the English spelling of Chinese words. There are three popular systems for transliterating Chinese characters into English—Yale, Wade-Giles, and Pin Yin. I know and use all three systems, thus, the mixture. If only one system was used exclusively, then I would favor it, but you will find many people who only use Wade-Giles, and just as many who are familiar with Pin Yin, etc. So, I offer you this key. To keep it simple, I will only explain the consonants.

Ch'	=	Ch
Ch	=	J
J	=	J
P'	=	P

P	=	B
B	=	B
K'	=	K
K	=	G
G	=	G
T'	=	T
T	=	D
D	=	D
X	=	Sh
Hs	=	Sh
Sh	=	Sh (Actually, Hs and Sh are slightly different, but difficult to teach to those unaccustomed to the language)
Tz	=	Hard Z
Ts	=	Hard S
Dz	=	Like the "ds" in adds
Zh	=	Hard J

No. 1

Ren

Zhong

Ren Zhong—This is point 26 on the Governing Vessel Meridian in acupuncture, located on the philtrum, the vertical groove on the midline of the upper lip. A heavy blow here can produce a serious sequelae of maxillary fractures, with the possibility of cardiac arrest, sudden inhibition of respiratory movements and possible suffocation.

No. 2

You

Bi

Ch'iao

You Bi Ch'iao—Right Nostril

No. 3

You

Sai

Chia

You Sai Chia—Right Cheek

No. 4

You

Yen

Bao

Yen

Jing

You Yen Bao Yen Jing—Right Eye and Socket

No. 5

You

Erh

Ch'ui

You Erh Ch'ui—Right Ear Lobe

No. 6

You

Erh

Ch'iao

You Erh Ch'iao—Right Ear Hole. This point is marked as fatal.

No. 7

You

Erh

Lun

You Erh Lun—Right Ear Wheel (Helix). It should be noted that behind the ear, hemorrhages in the brain tissue and between its membranes will result. Subarachnoid hematoma is fatal.

No. 8

You

Erh

You Erh—Right Ear

No. 9

You

Mei

You Mei—Right Eyebrow

No. 10

You

T'ai

Yang

T'ai Yang is a point located on the temple on each side. It is marked fatal because a heavy blow will cause skull fractures along the fontanelles, resulting in subarachnoid hematoma.

No. 11

You

E

Jiao

You E Jiao—Right Forehead Angle means the right temple and is marked as a fatal point for the same reasons as T'ai Yang.

No. 12

Mei

Ts'ung

Mei Ts'ung—The Crowding Together of the Eyebrows.

No. 13

P'ien

You

P'ien You—Leaning Right. This point is marked fatal. This may well be the topmost curving of the skull before reaching the level point at the very top. Fractures to the fontanelles will cause hemorrhages in the brain.

No. 14

Ding

Xin

Ding Xin —Top of the Mind. This is the top of the skull and is marked fatal. It would correspond to Bai Hui, point 20 on the Governing Vessel Meridian, and would result in hemorrhages in the brain.

No. 15

P'ien

Dzwe

P'ien Dzwe—Leaning Left. This is the same as number 13 P'ien You.

No. 16

E

Lu

E Lu—The Forehead. This point is marked fatal and would correspond to Sheng Ting, point 24 on the Governing Vessel Meridian.

No. 17

The same as number 11, but on the left side. This point is marked fatal.

No. 18
The same as number 10, but on the left side. This point is marked fatal.

No. 19
The same as number 9, but on the left side.

No. 20
The same as number 8, but on the left side.

No. 21
The same as number 7, but on the left side.

No. 22
The same as number 6, but on the left side. This point is marked fatal.

No. 23
The same as number 5, but on the left side.

No. 24
The same as number 4, but on the left side.

No. 25
The same as number 3, but on the left side.

No. 26
The same as number 2, but on the left side.

No. 27

Bi

Juen

Bi Juen—Tip of the Nose

No. 28

Hsin

Men

Hsin Men—Means the "Gate to the part of the head from the top to the forehead". This point is not an acupuncture point. It refers to the anterior fontanelle. Concussive vibration would cause bleeding in the brain tissue and subarachnoid hemorrhages; there could also be fractures of the skull. This point is marked fatal.

No. 29

Bi

Liang

Bi Liang—Bridge of the Nose

No. 30

You

Ling

Hai or Ke

You Ling Hai—Right neck to the chin. Along the side of the neck is the Carotid Sinus, which controls blood flow to the brain.

No. 31

Ch'ih

She

Ch'ih She—Juncture of the Teeth and Tongue. This point is marked fatal. It should be noted here that ancient coroners were instructed to note the teeth and tongue. "If it is a case of suicide by hanging, is the tongue pressed against the teeth or not?"

No. 32

Shih

Ch'i

Sang

Shih Ch'i Sang—The Throat

No. 33

You

Hsieh

P'en

No. 34

You

Jian

Jia

You Hsieh P'en—Right Super-clavicular Fossa. This point corresponds with point 12 on the Stomach Meridian, Ch'ueh Fen, just above the clavicle. Ch'ueh Fen is fatal.

You Jian Jia—Right Shoulder

No. 35
The same as number 34, but on the left side.

No. 36
The same as number 33, but on the left side.

No. 37

Yen

Hou

Yen Hou—The Larynx. This point is marked fatal. Located above the sternum, at the throat, a strike in the Adam's Apple region may lead to vertical fracture of the thyroid cartilage accompanied by hemorrhages from the carotid artery and the carotid sinus. There may also be sudden vagal inhibition with consequent cardiac arrest.

No. 38

Shang

Hsia

Ch'un

Ch'ih

Shang Hsia Ch'un Ch'ih—Upper and lower Lips and Teeth.

No. 39
The same as number 30, but on the left side.

No. 40

Hsiung

T'ang

Hsiung T'ang—The Chest. This point is marked fatal.

No. 41

You

Ru

You Ru—Right Nipple. This point is marked fatal. In acupuncture, this point is contra-indicated, in other words, it is dangerous to insert a needle here.

No. 42

Dzwe

Ru

Dzwe Ru—The Left Nipple. Same as number 41.

No. 43

Hsin or Xin

K'an

Hsin K'an—This is the indentation at the sternal notch on the breast. It is marked fatal. Results would be vagal inhibition (heart stoppage). There could also be damage to the coeliac plexus, to the liver, and hemorrhage from the coeliac artery.

No. 43 A

右　You

腋　Yeh

枳　Chi

You Yeh Chi—Right Armpit

No. 43 B

左　Dzwe

腋　Yeh

際　Chi

Dzwe Yeh Chi—Left Armpit

No. 44

右　You

肋　Lei or Le

You Lei—Right Ribs

No. 45

左　Dzwe

肋　Lei or Le

Dzwe Lei— Left Ribs

No. 46

肚
腹

Du

Fu

Du Fu—Stomach. This point is marked fatal.

No. 47

臍

Ch'i

Ch'i—Navel. This point is marked fatal. The Navel is a point contraindicated in acupuncture.

No. 48

右
肋

You

Hsieh

You Hsieh—Right Ribs. This is marked fatal. The Lei are the upper portion of the ribs, the Hsieh are the lower.

No. 49

左
肋

Dzwe

Hsieh

Dzwe Hsieh—Left Ribs. This is marked fatal.

No. 50

Xiao

Fu

小腹

Xiao Fu—The lower part of the abdomen below the umbilicus. This point is marked fatal. It corresponds with point 5 of the Conception Vessel Meridian, Shih Men, which is synonymous with Tan Tien, a contra-indicated point in acupuncture.

No. 51 A

Nan

Tzu

男子

Nan Tzu—A Man. This identifies the chart as either points to look for on a man or woman.

No. 51 B

Shen

Tzu

腎子

Shen Tzu—Testicles

No. 51 C

Shen

Nang

腎囊

Shen Nang—Scrotum

63

No. 51 D

Jing

Wu

Jing Wu—Penis

No. 51 E

Fu

Ren

Ch'an

Men

Fu Ren Ch'an Men—Female Vagina (This refers to a married woman).

No. 51 F

Ch'uh

Tzu

Yin

Hu

Ch'uh Tzu Yin Hu—Female Vagina (This refers to a virgin).

No. 52

You

K'ua

You K'ua—Right Side of the Groin.

No. 53

The same as number 52, but on the left side.

No. 54

右 You

腿 T'ui

You T'ui—Right Leg

No. 55

The same as number 54, but on the left side.

No. 56

右 You

膝 Hsi

You Hsi—Right Knee

No. 57

The same as number 56, but on the left side.

No. 58

右 You

臁 Lian

肋 Fen

You Lian Fen—Right Edge of the Calf

No. 59

The same as number 58, but on the left side.

No. 60

You

Chiao

Wan

You Chiao Wan—Right Ankle

No. 61

The same as number 60, but on the left side.

No. 62

You

Chiao

Mien

You Chiao Mien—Right Instep

No. 63

The same as number 62, but on the left side.

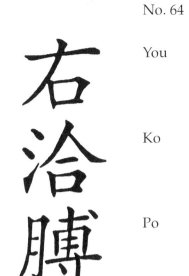

No. 64

You

Ko

Po

You Ko Po—Right Shoulder

No. 65
The same as number 64, but on the left side.

No. 66

You

Ch'ü

Ch'iu

You Ch'ü Ch'iu—The Point at the Crook of the Elbow.

No. 67
The same as number 66, but on the left side.

No. 68

You

Shou

Wan

You Shou Wan—Right Wrist

No. 69
The same as number 68, but on the left side.

No. 70

You

Shou

Xin

You Shou Xin—Right Center of the Palm

No. 71
The same as number 70, but on the left side.

 No. 72

You

Wu

Chih

You Wu Chih—Right Five Fingers

No. 73
The same as number 72, but on the left side.

 No. 74

You

Wu

Chih

Du

You Wu Chih Du—Right Undersides of the Five Fingers

No. 75
The same as number 74, but on the left side.

No. 76

You

Wu

Chih

Chia

Feng

You Wu Chih Chia Feng—Right Five Fingernails

No. 77
The same as number 76, but on the left side.

No. 78

You

Wu

Chih

Chia

You Wu Chih Chia—Right Five Toenails

No. 79
The same as number 78, but on the left side.

No. 80

You

Wu

Chih

You Wu Chih—Right Five Toes

No. 81
The same as number 80, but on the left side.

No. 1

Hou

Nao

Hou Nao—Rear Brain. The hind brain consisting of the cerebellum and medulla oblongata. This point is marked fatal.

No. 2

You

Erh

Gen

You Erh Gen—The Organ of Hearing (in Buddhism). This point is marked fatal.

No. 3
The same as number 2, but on the left side.

No. 4

Fa

Chi

Fa Chi—Hairline

No. 5

Jing

Ding

Jing Ding—Top of the Neck

No. 6

Bei

Chi

Bei Chi—The Spinal Column. This point is marked fatal.

No. 7
The same as number 6.

No. 8

You

Hou

Le

You Hou Le—Right Back of Ribs

No. 9
The same as number 8, but on the left side.

No. 10-11
These points are marked non-fatal, bear no names, and are a continuation of number 7.

No. 12

右後脅

You

Hou

Hsieh

You Hou Hsieh—Right back sides of the trunk from the armpits to the ribs. This point is marked fatal.

No. 13
The same as number 12, but on the left side.

No. 14

右腰眼

You

Yao

Yen

You Yao Yen—Right Yao Yen. This point is marked fatal.

No. 15
The same as number 14, but on the left side.

No. 16-17
These points are marked non-fatal, bear no names, and are a continuation of number 7.

No. 18

You

Shou

Wan

You Shou Wan—Right Wrist

No. 19

The same as number 18, but on the left side.

No. 20

You

Shou

Bei

You Shou Bei—Right Back of the Hand

No. 21

The same as number 20, but on the left side.

No. 22

You

T'un

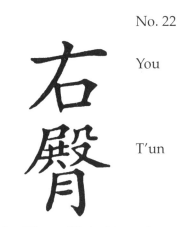

You T'un—Right Buttock

No. 23

The same as number 22, but on the left side.

No. 24

You

T'ui

You T'ui—Right Leg

No. 25

The same as number 24, but on the left side.

No. 26

Ku

Tao

Ku Tao—Anal Tract

No. 27

You

Chi

Lü

You Chi Lü—Right Spine (Right side)

No. 28
The same as number 27, but on the left side.

No. 29

You

Bei

Bo

You Bei Bo—Right Arm (Generally from the shoulders to the elbow)

No. 30
The same as number 29, but on the left side.

75

No. 31

You

Ge

Jou

You Ge Jou—Right Arm (Generally from the elbow to the wrist)

No. 32
The same as number 31, but on the left side.

No. 33

You

Ch'ü

Ch'iu

You Ch'ü Ch'iu—Right Crook of the Knee

No. 34
Same as 33, but on the left side.

No. 35

You

T'ui

Du

You T'ui Du—Right Calf

No. 36

Same as number 35, but on the left side.

No. 37

You

Jiao

Huai

You Jiao Huai—Right Ankle

No. 38

Same as number 37, but on the left side.

No. 39

You

Wu

Chih

You Wu Chih—Right Five Fingers

No. 40

Same as number 39, but on the left side.

No. 41

You

Wu

Chih

Chia

You Wu Chih Chia—Right Five Fingernails

No. 42
Same as number 41, but on the left side.

No. 43

You

Jiao

Gen

You Jiao Gen—Right Heel

No. 44
Same as number 43, but on the left side.

No. 45

You

Jiao

Xin

You Jiao Xin—Right Center (Arch) of the Foot

No. 46
Same as number 45, but on the left side.

No. 47

You

Wu

Ji

You Wu Ji—Right Five Toes

No. 48
Same as number 47, but on the left side.

No. 49

You

Wu

Ji

Du

You Wu Ji Du—Right Undersides of the Five Toes

No. 50
Same as number 49, but on the left side.

No. 51

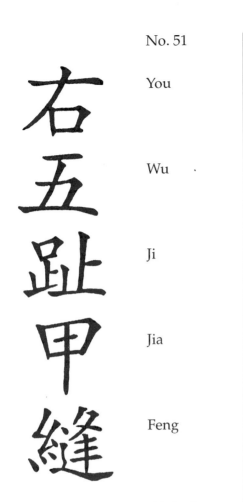

You

Wu

Ji

Jia

Feng

You Wu Ji Jia Feng—Cleft, Suture, or Crack of the Right Five Toenails

No. 52
Same as number 51, but on the left side.

T'ai—Great

Yang—Positive

T'ai Yang—Located in the temporal depression, about one inch behind the space between the end of the eyebrow and the outer canthus.

Usually, small-hand techniques are used against this point to compress a greater amount of pounds per square inch on the point. The palm may also be used, however. The results of a strike to this point will vary from dizziness to sudden death depending on the intensity of the strike.

Shan—Bloody smell

Jung—Center

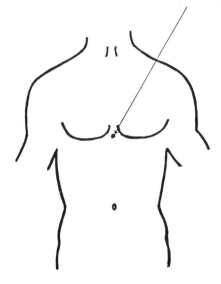

Shan Jung—Located on the sternal notch. A strike here can cause heart stoppage. If the force from the strike travels deep, there could also be damage to a number of important structures just below the diaphragm in this epigastric region. The coeliac (or solar) plexus, largest of the sympathetic plexuses, lies at about the level of the first lumbar vertebra, and there could be damage to the liver and hemorrhage from the coeliac artery.

Notes on the Point of Shan Jung

Shan Jung is also seen spelled two other ways—Shan Chung and Shan Zhong. Depending on how this point is struck, such as a full iron palm strike or small-hand technique, the results can vary from chest pain and angina pectoris, myocardial infarction. An understanding of these medical terms is in order here.

Angina Pectoris—A severe pain caused by shortage of oxygen in the heart muscle. Like any other muscle, the heart needs a supply of oxygen in proportion to the work it is doing, and the supply depends on the rate of flow in the arteries. The blood pumped through the heart is useless to the muscle, because the chambers of the heart have waterproof linings. Two small branches of the aorta, the coronary arteries distribute oxygenated blood to the heart muscle. If the work of the heart increases, more fuel (fat and sugar) is burned: more oxygen is taken up and more carbon dioxide is formed in exchange. The increased concentration of carbon dioxide makes the coronary arteries relax and admit more blood. In healthy people, the flow of blood to the heart muscle keeps pace with demand.

If the demand for oxygen is greater than the supply, the heart cannot work efficiently, but it does not necessarily immediately fail. The combustion is incomplete (i.e., the conversion of fat and sugar to carbon dioxide and water stops at an intermediate stage, and some intermediate product irritates nerve endings in the heart, causing violent pain).

Healthy young arteries are flexible enough to maintain an adequate flow in ordinary circumstances. Angina means that the coronary arteries are not healthy. The predisposing disorder is atheroma, a degeneration of the lining of the arteries with loss of elasticity. Even with atheromatous coronary arteries, the heart works normally within a limited range of activity, but if the range is exceeded, the arteries cannot expand enough to provide the additional oxygen that is needed, and the patient has an attack of angina.

The immediate cause of angina is physical effort, excitement, or a heavy meal; in short, whatever makes the heart beat faster.

The capacity for useful work is further reduced by a shortage of oxygen in the air (high altitude), or by anaemia, which diminishes the amount of oxygen carried in the blood. Smoking has the same effect, because carbon monoxide in tobacco smoke replaces some of the oxygen in the blood. Smoking also contributes to the underlying arterial disease. In these conditions, the heart must work harder to provide the amount of oxygen. Excessive fat is a useless burden to the heart. Flabby, untrained muscles are inefficient and waste oxygen.

Myocardial Infarction—Blockage of blood supply to part of the myocardium (heart muscle).

Infarction—Congestion and blockage of a blood vessel on which a part of an organ depends, with death and scarring of the affected tissue. The segment of lost tissue may be called an infarct.

In general, if one artery is blocked, neighboring arteries, with communicating branches, take over the work. Infarction occurs in places where small arteries do not communicate with each other, such as the kidney; or where the arteries together supply enough blood for the whole organ, with little in reserve, as in the brain; or where alternative arteries to the blocked one are also unhealthy and cannot take over, as in middle-aged hearts. If one were to simulate coronary thrombosis (clotting in an artery in the heart muscle) by artificially closing an artery in a healthy heart, probably nothing untoward would happen, because other coronary vessels would suffice. Postmortem studies have shown that people who have died from other causes have at some time had a coronary thrombosis without symptoms.

Yao—The Waist

Yen—A Tiny Hole; An Opening

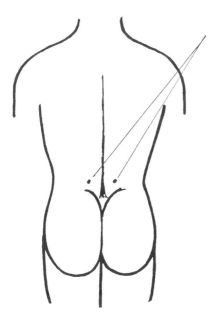

Yao Yen—Located low down on the back in the lumbar region on each side, not far from the lateral border of the sacro-spinalis muscle. Death will result from a strike of intense power.

Bai—Hundred

Hui—To Meet

Hundred Unity
Meeting Point for 100 Vessels
100 Meeting Point

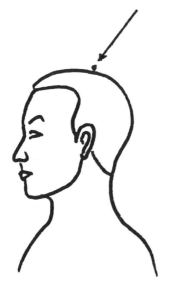

Bai Hui—Also, the Fontanelles of the Skull. Concussive vibration would cause bleeding in the brain tissue, and subarachnoid hemorrhages; there would also be fractures of the skull bones.

This point is located at Point 20 on the Governing Vessel Meridian, which is 5 tsun from the middle of the natural line of the hair above the forehead.

Nao—Brain

Hu—House Door

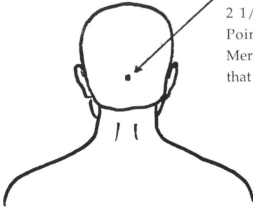

Nao Hu—This point is located about 2 1/2 tsun above the hairline, or Point 17 on the Governing Vessel Meridian. The effect is the same as that of hitting Bai Hui.

Arachnoid Membrane—The center membrane of the three that surround the brain and spinal cord (More details will follow).

Subarachnoid Hemorrhage—Bleeding into the subarachnoid space, that is, between the two innermost of the three membranes covering the brain. Symptoms are a sudden blinding, intense headache, rapidly followed by loss of consciousness and accompanied by profuse sweating. Coma and/or death could follow if not treated by opening the skull to relieve the pressure on the brain, removing the blood clot, and tying the artery.

Arachnoid Membrane—Arachne eidos, like a spider's web, so named for its extreme thinness, is a delicate membrane which envelops the brain, lying between the pia mater, internally, and the dura mater, externally. From this latter membrane it is separated by a space, the subdural space. It invests the brain loosely, being separated from direct contact with the cerebral substance by the pia mater, and a quantity of loose areolar tissue, the subarachnoidean. The arachnoid membrane surrounds the nerves which arise from the brain, and encloses them in loose sheathes as far as their point of exit from the skull.

The cerebro-spinal fluid fills up the subarachnoid space. It consists of 98.5 parts of water, with the remaining 1.5 percent being solid matter, animal and saline. It varies in quantity, being most abundant in the elderly, and is quickly reproduced. Its chief use is probably to afford mechanical protection to the nervous centers, and to prevent the effects of concussions communicated from without.

Fatal Points

Hsing Men
Hsin Kan
T'ai Yang
Yao Yen
Ta Hsing Men = Pai Hui
Hsiao Hsing Men = Hsing Hui or Shang Hsing
Ya Men
Feng Chi'ih

T'ien Chu
Wan Ku
Lien Ch'uan
Shan Chung
Yin Nang
Ch'ang Ch'iang
Chiu Wei
Chang Men
Shui Fen
Yin Tang
Ren Chung
Tan T'ien
Pai Hui
Shen Ting
Lu Hsi
Jen Ying
Ju Chung
Nao Hu
Feng Fu

Chapter Four
Meditation—
The Secrets of the Sacred

I am often asked by those who know that I am a kung-fu master if I know how to meditate. Usually they simply ask, "Do you meditate?", and that one question is more encompassing than they realize, for it is not one question that they have just asked, but several, and, therefore, there is no simple answer. You are now asking yourself how this can be, yet it is quite simple once you understand that meditation is simply directing one's thoughts totally to one function, and that this function can be anything from calming the mind to astral travel.

Since meditation is a door to a house, or a road to a destination, the beginning and the end result are often considered one. For instance, if I ask a monk from a monastery of the Catholic faith what he does when he meditates, he will likely say that he prays silently. If I ask a Tibetan lama the same question, he may, depending on the sect to which he belongs, say that he is enhancing the Skill of the Third Eye, the ability to see psychically. Think of meditation as a telephone wire leading into a business building. That wire seems to be just one wire to the untrained mind, but in fact, it is a bundle of wires which will ring many different phones inside that building, depending on which wire we select.

From Christian books of meditations, to Christian fanatics who think that people who meditate are Satan worshippers, the opinions on what meditation is and how it is approached are many. Most people who seek me out from the martial arts world are thinking of the picture of a Buddhist monk kneeling, or sitting in a cross-legged lotus position, eyes closed, back ramrod straight, concentrating on his breathing. So when they ask me if I meditate, I usually assume that this is the limit of their question and go no further. But there are those who have a more extensive knowledge of meditation and its many destinations, and they want me to tell them more than I tell the average person. What I tell them about meditation is the subject of this chapter.

The abilities that can be reached through the study of meditation will sound like a list of fantasy tales, but I am known for my integrity, and I list these not as an attempt at sensationalism, but with the thought of educating the inquiring student as to the abilities that exist.

Simple meditation calms the mind and helps the practitioner channel his thoughts to the need at hand, such as supreme serenity. But complex meditation leaves that level and goes on to a higher one of more diverse capabilities. With higher levels of meditation it is possible to travel outside the body to destinations of time and space, even to the plane of existence beyond death. Some advanced meditative skills render the practitioner passive, others active; it should come as no surprise when you see someone sitting still and practicing one type of meditation and another who walks on hot coals of fire while wrapping himself in chains which have been heated white hot.

I have watched as men stuck needles the size of bicycle spokes through their noses, through one side of the right cheek and out the other side of the left cheek, pulled their tongues out and stuck these needles through them so that the tongues could not be withdrawn into their mouths until they arrived at the temple to which they were walking. While they were self-impaled they were pulling carts laden with sacrifices to their deities. The carts then were pulled with ropes attached to large hooks which, in turn, were imbedded in their bare backs. It goes without saying that this is very active meditation.

There are lamas in Tibet who can raise the temperature of their bodies at will, so that, during their initiation, they are required to thaw a robe that has been dipped in ice water and wrapped around their naked bodies. To make matters worse, this initiation ceremony takes place on an extremely cold and blustery night, high in the mountains of Tibet. Yet, these monks remain until their robes have dried.

I have personally seen objects moved with no physical contact and have read documented accounts of levitation. There is a meditation skill in Tibet called "lung gom", in which the adept can cover unbelievable distances without stopping for rest, food, or water, and when I say unbelievable distances, try to imagine running 50-to-60 hours! It is amazing to think of all the abilities the human mind and body is capable of, and, yet, remain unharnessed.

There is a meditation skill that is familiar to some circles of kung-fu practitioners called "Circulating the Dragon's Breath". This skill allows the adept to emit a force that cannot be seen, yet can be felt with a strong impact from several feet away. It is usually emitted from the open palms. I once heard of an old man in Chinatown, San Francisco, who could hit someone with this skill from a distance of 12 feet. While I never had the good fortune of personally watching him demonstrate, I was taught this skill by a friend from Indonesia years ago, and back when I used to practice it, I personally experienced the phenomenon of this force leaving my body.

"Circulating the Dragon's Breath" is learned by levels, and I should warn those of you who would go too far too soon that racing ahead with this skill can bring about serious injury. My teacher told me of a friend's uncle who was a monk in a nearby temple. He was a practitioner of this skill and was found dead one morning at the temple. Found sitting in the meditative posture, he was bleeding from the eyes, ears, nose and mouth. There was no doubt in anyone's mind that he had been practicing and had managed to burst every blood vessel in its path by circulating the Dragon's Breath in the wrong direction. What frightening consequences! With that story fresh in our minds, let us see if we can acquire this skill.

The first step is learning to calm the mind and follow prescribed paths with thought. Sitting in a cross-legged lotus or kneeling position, the back kept straight, the head erect, eyes closed (only at advanced stages are the eyes kept open), the practitioner breathes in through the nose, and imagines the breath going in a line up over the top of the brain, down the back of the head, down the back of the neck, and on down the back until it reaches the waist. Then he exhales, and the breath now continues on a line from the bottom at a point several inches below the navel called the Tan Tien. As he exhales, the breath goes from the Tan Tien up the front of the chest, up the front of the throat and face, and exits through the nose. This is one cycle; inhale, exhale.

Level One

At level one, merely concentrate on inhaling and literally envisioning that path over the top of the head and down the back; then, exhaling and seeing the path from the Tan Tien to the nose. See this path with the mind's eye as if you can see inside yourself. Traverse that entire route with your mind as if you were tracing it with your finger. Let nothing break your concentration, and when you finish, it is with the exhalation, not the inhalation.

Level Two

Level two becomes more of a challenge. Here, one must now see the entire path of the inhalation/exhalation as one loop or circle. There are now no stopping points until one finishes the exercise with the final exhalation. As I said, one must now think of one continuous loop. Begin by inhaling and seeing the entire path filled with the breath, as water fills a pipe. Fill the entire path with breath and see the entire path, not just one part of it. This is important. One must be able to see not only the entire path—all at the same time—but the breath flowing through it as well. Then the inhaling and exhaling becomes no longer the starting and stopping points that they were at level one, but merely intake and exhaust. The path, the flow, and the ability to mentally see it in its entirety is the key to this level. When one can see the path as a loop in its entirety, then he is ready for level three.

Level Three

At level three, we depart from the nose as the initiating point and head for the Tan Tien. Mentally look inside yourself in the direction of this point, which is about three inches below the navel. Imagine a small white ball of energy, or light, sitting there, looking like a miniature version of the sun. Now imagine its movement to be like the breath which you learned to circulate in level one. It is a ball of enfolding energy which you control. Now, while keeping this ball of energy in sight at all times, pull a loop from the top of it and have that loop extend upward into your chest. The loop must have energy coming from the ball, traveling the entire path, and returning to the ball. There must be no breaks in the loop; the ball of energy, and the loop and its flow, must be seen at all times. To end the exercise, return the loop to the ball of energy, then let the ball fade until extinguished. Never just cut it off, since this is supposedly powerful enough to burst blood vessels. You will, at some point, be dealing with literal energy flow during study at this level.

Level Four

Level four takes us to directing the energy out of the body. Sitting in your usual meditative posture, place your palms together in front of your chest, and, while holding them together, pull the loop of energy from the ball of white light which you now envision in the Tan Tien. Pull the loop up into the chest, keeping full control to ensure you see all in its entirety. (If you cannot see the entire ball of energy and, at the same time, the energy's flow around the loop, you are not ready to go beyond this point.) Now begin to pull the sides of the loop into your arms so that the path looks like a "T" of flowing energy. Continue to extend the ends of the loop into the arms until the ends of the loop reach the palms. Think beyond the palms and, at that point, you will experience a force that will literally push your palms apart. When it pushes the palms apart, you no longer need my help. You have successfully circulated the Dragon's Breath.

The Mountain

You have asked me to tell you about the mountain. Some of you have even begged me to tell you about the mountain. Whether you ask or beg, I will not tell you, but if you trully ask I will try to tell you. If I tell I will not see it. If I take you to see it, you will not hear what I have to say.

If, as I tell you about the mountain, I tell you about the trees that grow on its banks, the beautiful trees that seem to grow forever in awesome oneness with the sky, and you suddenly say, "Ah! I know now what the mountain looks like," you will go and teach trees, and those whom you teach will not see the mountain for the trees.

If, as I tell you about the mountain, I tell you about the beautiful streams that cascade down its side, streams that seem to carry the conversations of the sages on their rushing tongues, and you suddenly say, "Ah! I know what the mountain looks like, " you will go and teach streams, and those whom you teach will build rafts.

If, as I tell you about the mountain, I tell you about the caves I discovered while climbing its heights, the deep caves filled with wonderful silence and solemnity, and you suddenly say, "Ah! I know what the mountain looks like," you will go and teach caves, and those whom you teach will dig holes and become old men.

If, as I tell you about the mountain, I tell you about the mountain's peak, how it scrapes the sky with god-like power for all its towering splendor, yet is at one with all around it, and you suddenly say, "Ah! I know now what the mountain looks like," you will go and teach the mountaintops, and those whom you teach will call themselves teachers.

If you truly ask me to tell you, I will tell you where I went and how; I will point the way, but I will not be your hands and feet. If you ask me how fast I ran to find the mountain, I will not tell you. If you truly ask me where the mountain may be found, I will point to the path. If you ask me how hard it was to climb, my ears will hear the conversation of ants with the deer, and the songs of butterfly wings. If you hear these things, you have been to the mountain.

Some blind themselves, while some blind others, and there are even those who blind themselves while blinding others. They blind by demanding to be recognized as part of the mountain, but when they have gone, the trees will grow on, the caves will solemnize for centuries to come, the streams will still speak wisdom, and the mountain's peak will still draw a line between heaven and earth. I have been to the mountain and found I could not speak. I could only point and hear.

12:35 a.m. February 2, 1983

In Search of the Perfect Apple

"Are we allowed to eat apples?" he asked. "Are they not the 'forbidden fruit'?" The youthful eyes, full of sincerity and honesty, looked pleadingly into mine and awaited not an answer, but the unquestionable truth. This youth have been told many things about the apple, but had never spoken to anyone who knew for sure, and many had said that the apple could kill. Some had even said that only a bite and one would die. Thus, just an answer would do. No. It must be the undeniable truth.

The fear in this youth is not from what he does not know, but from what he knows. He knows more than some, less than others, but most of all he does not know that he does not know the truth, for he has been told that the truth is there for all to know if one will only take the apple and eat it.

"What do you know of the apple?" I asked.

The youth spoke. "I have seen the apple go from green to red. I believe what I have seen."

"What you have seen, you have seen," I said. "What do you know?"

"Once, a friend I know ate some apples, and the next day when I awoke, he was dead," the youth said in great sincerity.

"A lie has no taste," I said, "and your friend was killed by the truth." "What do you know of the apple?"

He answered, "I know that I fear it. I fear that I have only one life and only one choice. I fear what that choice will do to that one life."

"Then live more than one life," I said, "for I am not the apple."

The youth cried, "I have only one life to live!"

"Then," I said, "you must eat the perfect apple."

"Where can I find the perfect apple?" he asked.

I answered, "It grows where you have not looked, on trees untouched by the hands of man. Never on a low branch, always up high. If you do not seek to find the perfect apple, then when you see it, it will be a dark snake on a golden pond. Kill the snake and the apple will appear. I warn you , if you see the snake and let it live, you will go blind."

"Master," said the youth, "what is this snake on a golden pond? Where is it, and why have I not seen it?"

"The snake on the golden pond is the guardian of your fears, and the golden pond is the beauty of mystery. Where it is, is known only to you, for though you say you have not seen it, without your eyes I could not have described it."

"Master," he pleaded, "I wish with all my heart to find the perfect apple. Where may I find it?"

I replied, "The distance from here to the tree upon which grows the perfect apple is very short, but the travel is so difficult as to be impossible for some."

"What must I do to take this journey?" he asked.

"You must remove the stone that you have been balancing on your shoulder," I said. There was an alarmed look on his face.

"Master, I cannot do that. The stone I balance on my shoulder is the way my friends and I find a common interest. Without it, we would be unable to be friends."

"The stone is very heavy and cuts into your skin," I said.

"Yes, but I must keep it if I am to be accepted by my friends. Why some of them even have stones bigger than mine and are bent nearly double by the weight. I must keep mine."

I replied, "Did I not tell you the distance was short but the journey difficult? Put off your stone."

Sadly, he walked away keeping the stone balanced on his shoulder. "I'll find another path, or an easier way," he said.

"Your heart was not pure in the desire to find it," I whispered, and, with that I ate the apple I was holding in my hand.

3:00 a.m. Sunday, December 28, 1986

Tell Me, Humble One

I saw the man passing by me, and though he seemed to look my way, I knew he could not see me, for he had only one eye, and it was turned inward. Not having the ability to look outward, away from himself, he saw only himself, yet was quite content to be this way. "What I cannot see cannot be any loss," he said.

"I am a doctor," I told him. "Perhaps I could operate." But, when I said this, his ears fell off.

The cave echoes, because there are not people to fill its emptiness, and all the screams from time memorial will not remove the emptiness.

"Talk to me," he said, but I knew words would be wasted on a man with no ears. When he could not hear me, he began to sing a song about his life. It comforted him so much that he did not care that his ears were gone.

I discovered later that he was a pilgrim, like myself, on the way to the great Festival, a place where many happy, friendly people gather. However, his second eye, the one that looks outward, never developed, and he ended up singing his songs in the cave called "Important."

2:38 a.m. January 20, 1989

The Poet Whispers

Sit thee still and hear, Young Man, for in thine ears
I pour the winds of yesterday.
They were the same that once did blow
upon the ashes of this bard who stretches out to whisper now
and tread upon thy golden shore.
Thou thinkest me dead, yet readest thou these lines I've writ to thee,
for in this love of which I speak,
there is a moonlit sea to which we both have come,
compelled by mysteries I sought to name.
Stars cannot be held within the hands, and moons upon the ocean stay,
yet how will pen we would rewrite the very universe,
If we could only have the one we love.
I failed and wrote, you read and weep,
as reeds upon the bank do bend in midnight breeze
and honour, thus, the passing of a time;
and you shall be like me and write of love you sought,
of all its temples and its families.
You shall carve my poem in the mountain just to fill it in with dirt
when last this flame has flickered;
born of hope, t'was destined more to die,
yet from its death there tolls a bell that shall ring on for thee.
Throughout the time of coming years
and bending reeds on moon-hushed banks,
shall moonlit oceans call to read young lovers like yourself.
And some shall be, and some shall not, but let that be.
Love thou deep, and love thou well,
and then record it thus as I have spoke to thee,
that on the leaves of summer's love the winds of yesterday may blow.

2:13 a.m. October 12, 1989